The Missing Pieces To Your Home Business

The Information You Need To Succeed!

By

Michele Beauvoir, MBA

Published by Nomad CEO Publishing

ISBN-13:978-1492878469

Legal Disclaimer

Disclaimer and Terms of Use: The Author and Publisher have strived to be as accurate and complete as possible in the creation of this book, notwithstanding the fact that she does not warrant or represent at any time that the contents within are accurate due to the rapidly changing nature of the Internet. While all attempts have been made to verify information provided in this publication, the Author and Publisher assumes no responsibility for errors, omissions, or contrary interpretation of the subject matter herein. Any perceived slights of specific persons, peoples, or organizations are unintentional. In practical advice books, like anything else in life, there are no guarantees of income made. Readers are cautioned to rely on their own judgment about their individual circumstances to act accordingly. This book is not intended for use as a source of legal, business, accounting or financial advice. All readers are advised to seek services of competent professionals in the legal, business, accounting, and finance fields.

Send all inquiries to
McBOV REI, Inc
PO Box 582
Belvidere, IL 61008

Dedication

This book is dedicated to my family and friends for all their support throughout the development of this book. I especially dedicate this book to my mother, who continually inspires me to reach for the stars; my sister Nadege Beauvoir for always being honest; and my grandmother for her firm belief in education.

Preface

My name is Michele Beauvoir, and the purpose of this book is to reach out to anyone who is considering starting a small business, home-based business, or online business.

This book is the product of my personal experience. I was not always a successful entrepreneur. There was a time when I was clueless, and my thoughts and ideas were scattered.

In 2005, I took a two-month trip to Gonaïve, Haiti, to help Ebenezer Missions in translation and public relations. I went there with only two hundred dollars in cash, and it was one of the most challenging things I've ever done. Upon my return to my hometown of Chicago, Illinois, I received a stipend of $1,000 from Ebenezer Missions. This financial support allowed me to embark on a new journey. I studied many business books about successful entrepreneurs who had made fortunes in real estate investments and other business areas. I was inspired to become an entrepreneur, and over the years I tried and failed at many businesses.

Then I learned the nine key lessons that follow. These nine lessons helped change my life, and they can help you, too:

1. **Learn How to Invest Profitably**

   The best way to do this is to read books, go to seminars, get a mentor(s), or join a club. During that time in 2006 after I had returned from Haiti, I read books on real estate, stocks, securities, and business start-ups. My first investment acquisition was in Kansas City, Missouri—two houses and two parcels of land.

2. **Become Familiar with the Internet**

   The Internet provides many opportunities for business, and those who bear with it can reap massive profits. I purchased several ebooks that explain how to make money, how to create web software, and how to build websites and manipulate html sources.

3. **Learn Good Writing and Editing Skills**

   Good writing and editing skills are not easy to maintain unless you make a habit of reading books regularly, even daily. The way I managed to do this was by making a decision to read well-written books and published essays, and even by listening to audio books. Listening to them allowed me to memorize many esteemed writing pieces. Once I became confident in my new skills, I wrote this book.

4. **Learn How to Sell**

   A sale will always be made, whether by you or someone else. In other words, imagine your everyday conversations, social settings, interviews, work demands, and such. Haven't you noticed by now that a sale will always be made? I knew I had to make a decision to change what I had been doing in order to get different results.

5. **Be Creative and Innovative**

   Creativity and innovation often go hand in hand with success. Think about the creation of great companies like Microsoft and Apple, or advances like cell phones and the Internet—the list goes on to show the importance and benefits of taking the time to invent something. My experiences will tell you that this is not an easy path to take. It takes trial and error and risk-taking to see this through.

One principle I learned much later in my journey from the book *The Science of Getting Rich* by Wallace Wattles is that rich or successful people do things in a certain way, and anyone who follows that particular way of doing things can get similar results. In short, if you know what you want to achieve, become obsessed with it, think of it day and night, and do the best you can where you are now, then what you've done is actually set yourself up for success in order to prepare yourself to receive your desires. In other words, you are aligning yourself to success.

6. **Join Networks and Associations**

   Networks and associations are useful because not only can you build valuable relationships, but you can learn what others already know. Furthermore, you are setting yourself up for success by associating with people who have the same purpose and similar goals.

7. **Learn Business and Tax Law**

   One thing I'm convinced of is that knowledge is power, and ignorance is *not* bliss. The more you understand the laws as they relate to your particular business, the more money you get to keep in your pocket when it comes to preventing unnecessary fines, penalties, and lawsuits.

8. **Have a Burning Desire for Goals**

   A burning passion is the essence of success because it will allow you to overcome any obstacle, ridicule, and challenge along your journey to success. So keep the fire burning and smile away.

9. **Read Daily and Learn New Ideas**

   This is one of the hardest parts to be faithful to, but those who persevere may become authors and experts.

McBov.info provides a vast amount of information to stimulate entrepreneurial creativity. We support and encourage investment strategies in real estate and business start-ups.

Table of Contents

Introduction

Today is the first day of the rest of your new life. Why? Because by choosing to read this book it tells me that (1) you have already made up your mind to start your own business or (2) you've already started your business, but are stumped on what actions to take next. Whatever the case, I applaud you!

Believe it or not, there has never been a better time to start a business, especially a home-based business, than right now. During this recent recession, times have been extremely difficult for many. But the good news is that new businesses are popping up every day all across the country.

If you have been laid off or are barely making ends meet with the income you're currently receiving, but have a burning desire to turn your creative ideas into a business, then you're on the right track by simply reading this book. And this should not be the only one you read. I recommend several others. Simply go to your local bookstore, and you'll find them in the business section. As for me, most of the lessons learned in my journey stemmed from several role models, like Wallace Wattles in *The Science of Getting Rich*; Napoleon Hill in *Think and Grow Rich*; Emily Post in *Etiquette in Society*; Donald Trump; Ambrose Bierce; and many more.

For many people, a significant barrier to opening a new business is the cost. Many entrepreneurs simply don't have access to tens of thousands, or even hundreds of thousands of dollars, or don't want to go deeply into debt. Today, especially with the Internet, it's possible to start a profitable business with a very modest investment.

My objective is to reach out to those wanting to start a small business outside of the home using effective methods that would minimize cost and maximize profits. How can that be accomplished? For example: if you are thinking about opening a doctor's office for Chiropractors, Optometrist, etc., or starting a nursing school (CNA, LPN, RN), boutique, crafts, or dollar store, the first thing is to pick a high traffic location, like a business strip mall, popular hang-out locations, near universities, and such. Next, invest in effective sales training and recruit a group of young motivated people to conduct direct marketing on your behalf. Simple ideas with a low start-up cost, plus the potential to maximize profit.

The goal of this book is to provide you with a roadmap for starting your own business for $1,000 or less. Throughout this book you will learn key lessons and principles, like the example above that will help you along your path to success.

We want to help you get your business off to a good start. All of the information in the following chapters will help you to avoid the mistakes that many new start-ups make. But don't skip over any of the steps—even though your business can be successful on a tight budget, cutting corners can bring the whole structure tumbling down. Fortunately, both planning and dedication take the place of cash investments when building a business.

To Your Success,

Michele Beauvoir

Chapter 1

The Road to Happiness

The Road To Happiness

Congratulations! You are about to set sail on a new and exciting adventure of starting your own home based business.

Like any other brick and mortar or internet business, in order to be successful your new business will entail planning and preparation. Right about now you are probably so excited that you think just putting together a website is going to bring you thousands of clients.

Reality check!

Did you know that about 95 percent of startup businesses tend to fail within the first three years?

You're probably thinking, "Well, if those are the odds, then why should I even try?"

Now don't give up before you even start!

Most businesses fail because they don't have a plan. They have an *idea,* but they don't have any thought as to how they are going to make their idea work.

Let's use this as an example: You want to put a pool in your backyard, so you call the pool store and say "bring me a pool," right? Wrong! You need to know what size you want, where that pool is going to go, if it will be chlorine or salt, should it be heated, etc, etc, etc. You need to plan all this out before you can just throw a pool in the ground.

The same applies with a business. It needs to be planned out. There are steps that need to be taken, and most of the time they need to be in a certain order.

Building your home based business

Be honest with yourself. You don't want just a business. You want a

successful business, right? Well, I am here to tell you that with an open mind, and a little help, you can make your business as successful as you want it to be.

Running a home based business takes an entirely different frame of mind and skill set than working at a physical location. Most people already have a pre-conceived notion of those who work from home. They usually picture someone lying around on the couch all day in their nightgown or underwear, or hanging out by the pool in their bathing suit with their laptop and a cold one. (All right, Tuesdays is the only day I do that! ☺)

In reality, operating a home based business is much less glitzy. Just ask anyone who runs a business from home. The truth is that there are long hours, nonstop responsibilities, and hassles with clients that don't really happen in the "regular" business world.

But don't misunderstand me. It is also one of the most gratifying, enjoyable, satisfying and worthwhile things that you could ever do. And even if it is hard from the beginning, it does get easier as you move through. However, by being prepared and knowing all the facts about running your business before you even begin one, you can turn an impending catastrophe into one of the most rewarding and fulfilling careers you could ever dream of.

And who knows, maybe sooner than later you yourself will be lounging at the pool with a laptop and a cold one, and everyone will be asking <u>you</u> how you did it.

Strengths vs. Weaknesses

Take this short test to help you find where your strengths and weaknesses lie. Be totally honest with your answers; the truth will help you to find out what you need to work on to succeed in your business.

Answer each question with Yes or No. If they do not apply to you or your business, you may skip the question.

MOTIVATION

- Are you generally able to complete tasks at the office, housework, school projects with your children or home crafts, even when you don't feel like doing any of them?
- Is the main reason you want to run a company important to you? What about to your family?
- Can you stick with it through working twelve or fourteen hours or more straight, for multiple days in a row?
- Are you the type that will follow through on your ideas or projects you'd like to accomplish?

PERSONAL RESPONSIBILITY

- When you take on a project or task, do you consider it "yours", even if it fails?
- Are you the type of person that will own up to your mistakes?
- Would you try to find the owner and tell them what happened if you hit an empty car in a parking lot?
- Do you believe in the importance of insurance, whether it's a written contract between two parties, or a policy from an insurance company to protect your assets?

PASSION

- Are you able to talk confidently for hours on end about what you are doing, or plan to do? Can you do it without being boring?
- If you are currently working, do you love your job? Are you planning on starting your company in the same niche you are currently working in?

- If you need to work at a job for a limited time while running your business, will you be able to enjoy your job?
- If you could only work in one industry for the rest of your life, would you choose the one you're planning to start your business in?

SELF-DISCIPLINE

- Are you able to focus on the task at hand until it's completed?
- If you have unfinished business that needs to get done, is it easy for you to pass on an exciting invitation from friends and family?
- Are there things in your life, such as losing weight or saving money for a new car that you've accomplished by making a plan and following through?
- If you are in the middle of working on something important, are you able to resist checking Facebook or playing computer games?

DETERMINATION

- Can you negotiate at a garage sale or flea market if the price of an item you want is considered unreasonably high?
- Do people usually consider you stubborn? Do you refuse to let go until you get what you want?
- Would you do anything to get your business up and running successfully?
- If you are asked to carry out a task that you know you won't be able to get to in a reasonable amount of time, can you reply with a totally guilt-free "no?"

Now check your answers. If you answered "yes" to more questions in a particular section, then that is where your strengths lie. If you have more "no" entries, then these are the features that you will need to consider cultivating.

Character Traits

Now that you know your strengths and weaknesses, let's take a look at why these are important:

1) ***Motivation***
   There are thousands of reasons why people want to work from home. Some might include the challenge, the freedom, the potential money, spending more time with the family, no more commute, cutting down on expenses, not having to answer to another boss, boredom in retirement, etc. But no matter what your reason is, be sure that your motivation is strong enough when the "going gets tough."
2) ***Passion***
   Surprised? This is a tough trait to come by, because it is a hard one to keep. You'll be spending a lot of time imagining what you want your business to be, while also working on it, working in it, developing it and eventually persuading potential customers to actually become your clients. Your passion needs to come through because not only are you selling yourself, you're also selling your business, and this passion must come through as genuine, otherwise your customers will not be convinced that you are the right person to work with.
3) ***Self-discipline***
   The majority of new entrepreneurs naturally do not have the amount of self-discipline that is required to run a home-based business. But it can be learned and developed. Just keep in mind that you will not have any one to answer to, so the work won't get done unless you do it yourself. Also, temptation is just a step away: playing games on the computer, watching soap operas, shopping for 3 hours, having lunch with the

girls/guys, just to name a few. The more you do what you need to do, the more natural everything will become.

4) ***Fortitude***

   As you are starting your new business, let your family and friends know, because they will be your most probable interruptions. Yes, they mean well, but you cannot go running to the grocery store or take a walk in the park or go see a matinee at the drop of a hat. And if you constantly give in to distractions, you are never going to get your business off the ground, let alone keep it going. Having the fortitude to make your company successful will help you learn to say "no" to distractions, no matter how reasonable they may sound.

5) ***Accountability***

   Whatever goes right - or wrong - in your business, lies on your shoulders. You will be the person responsible for taking care of any good or bad issues that come up. That can be daunting at times. While at other times very rewarding, because you get to take all the credit for a job well done.

The gratification and self-respect that you will come to know in running a home based company is unparalleled to anything you have ever done before. So if you are still excited, keep reading. It only gets better from here!

Chapter 2

The Development Stage

If you are the laid-back type of person that is waiting for the money tree to shed its bills, you'll be old and grey before that happens! Money doesn't grow on trees, and entrepreneurs know that. Entrepreneurs are a different breed. They are hard working and dedicated, and once they set their minds to it, they find all sorts of ways to make their business successful. There are so many opportunities in this vast world outside of your couch, but it just takes perseverance, and a little bit of research.

Although most businesses will require a small amount of start-up capital, many businesses can be started with nothing, or next to nothing. If you carefully investigate your options, you will be able to find opportunities that will yield high returns. Where can you find these opportunities, you ask? Online, of course! The internet provides a tremendous amount of resources to help you find low cost business opportunities.

At the beginning of your search for that perfect business, careful and thorough research is needed, mostly so that you don't miss out on a great business opportunity. While researching the internet make a list of the ones that peak your interest, with a list of pros and cons. This will help you to choose the best business venture that will meet your needs.

Once you have your list in hand, ask yourself a few questions to help weed out the business opportunities that may not suit you:

1. Are you leaning more towards services, or products?
2. Do you have enough funds to get you started?
3. Which do you prefer – the quiet sanctity of an online business,

or a storefront where you can personally socialize with your customers?

4. Will you be seeking Joint Venture partners?
5. Does the market demand this business?

These are just a few of the questions that will need to be asked, and after you've answered them you should be able to choose which business venture appeals most to you and your personality. But keep in mind that even though the business chosen is “low cost,” you may still be able to earn high returns, with dedication and hard work.

Keep focused on your objectives and goals. You will be able to achieve financial success with the proper motivation and knowledge. Learn everything you can about the business itself, as well as the “behind the scenes” tasks that come along with the business, such as staffing, organizing, planning, controlling and financing.

Keep your attitude in check. The majority of successful entrepreneurs are thinkers, risk-takers, full of self determination and confident. Remain focused, and don’t get too discouraged when problems and challenges pop up.

So, are you ready to start looking for that perfect, low cost business opportunity? Just log in to the internet and all the resources will be there, right at your fingertips.

Take risks, have the right attitude and outlook, and you will be sure to produce and maintain a successful business.

Step By Step

Now that you have a few of the basics down, let’s talk about the type of business you want to develop. You may already know exactly what you want to do, or maybe you have so many different ideas running around in your head that you are dizzier than normal! Well, if you are one of the undecided ones, or the one that already knows but may be still sitting on the edge of the fence, here is a step-by-step process to hopefully help you decide:

First, write down your ideas on a blank sheet of paper, and separate

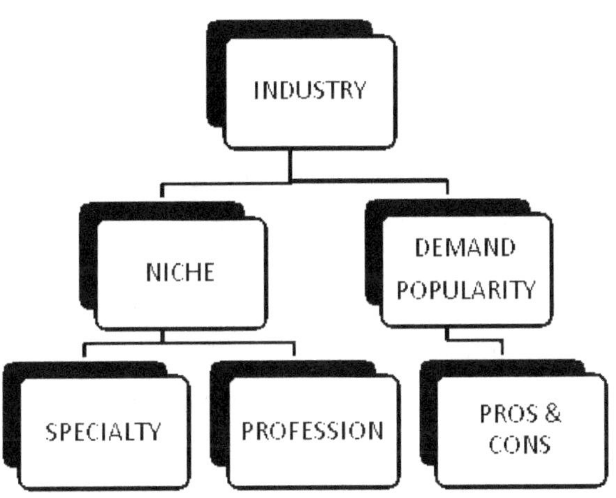

them into different categories.

For instance, start with the Industry that you want to be in and then go to Niche/Specialty. From there, determine your product's Profession, Demand/Popularity and the current Pros and Cons.

Confused? Let's just break this down a little more with the following example:

A. **Industry** – What is the main industry that you would like to work in? For this example we will use the *Food and Beverage* industry.

B. **Niche –** This is your specialty business within the industry, so let's choose *Home Bakery.*

C. **Demand/ Popularity –** Is this a good business that people will run to? How many other businesses are out there with the same idea? How are they working out? What is the main reason that this business will work? *Everyone loves baked goods*

D. **Specialty –** A home bakery is a broad category. Are you good at all baked items, or do you have one special goodie that is your signature, one that everyone craves when you make? *Cupcakes*

E. **Profession-** What background do you have that will be a big plus in doing this business? *Baker*

F. **Pros & Cons** - Pros - *Fewer bakeries in cities, more people are ordering from the internet, the cupcake business is starting to explode.* Cons – *High end equipment needed, shipping product so it stays fresh, can't be done alone.*

Next, write out a proposal by including *who* your product or services will target; *what* type of products or services you will provide and what sets them apart from the rest; and *when* you will officially launch it. The *where* question, the location of the main operation, addresses whether it will be from home, nationwide, or worldwide. The *how* part of the proposal will address how you market the business to generate sufficient revenue and provide a proposed funding source whether it is alone, with partners, or through the bank. The *why* explains the reason your particular business should be in existence in relation to its contribution to society as a whole.

Selecting a business is not as easy as it appears to be because there are several actions to consider, such as brainstorming, researching, product testing, projecting of sales potential, and considering competition atmosphere, to name a few. Hence, take your time and do your research. It may be wise to look into specializing in a small niche market to begin.

The simpler you keep your business, the higher its chances of survival and success. It's easy for entrepreneurs to choose a too-broad field of interest and thereby lose focus.

The **second** option is another way to brainstorm and determine what type of business would be feasible. It's called the process of "compare and contrast." Use this method if you want to remain under a certain start-up budget.

The following table is for example purposes only. Simply use the titles and formulate your creative ideas for an outlook on your potential:

TYPE OF BUSINESS	**START-UP COSTS**	**EARNING POTENTIAL**	**RISK LEVEL LOW/HIGH**
Cleaning Housekeeping Maintenance Hauling Window Washer	$100-$500 Initial Cost	$800-$4,000 /month for 8-40 houses at $100-$250 per day	Medium Risk Cautions: Need liability insurance and business license.
Writer Ghostwriter Editor Copy Writer	$50-$900 Initial Cost	$2,500-$10,000 / month for 1-3 clients at $2,500 to $5,000 per book/project	Low Risk Cautions: Finish projects promptly. Avoid plagiarism.
Mailer Marketing Envelope	$100-$900 Initial Cost	$500-$5,000 /month for 3-10 clients at $150-	Low Risk Cautions: Invasion of

Stuffing		$300 each	privacy and permit laws.
Home-Based: Child Daycare Group Daycare Adult Daycare	$900+ Initial Cost	$5000+/month for 6-10 clients.	Medium Risk Safety issues Home Maint.

Now let's take one example from each category and expand on it:

1) **Housecleaning:** The initial start up for a housecleaning business is fairly small, once you get your business license and liability insurance, which are a must. Some states even require bonding, but this is also a relatively small cost. Once you have that all in order, your next cost will be cleaning supplies: vacuums, brooms, mops, pails, glass cleaners, cloths, furniture polish, degreaser, etc. You can save a lot of money on these supplies by going to a store like the Dollar General, the Dollar Store or Wal-mart. A lot of clients will prefer that you use their own products, so the cost to you for their home would be $0.00. But let's say the initial cost of insurance, license, bonding and supplies breaks down to $100 per month. Get one client where you charge $100 per month, and you've already made your initial investment back. Any other customers after that is pure profit.
2) **Copy Writer** – Many entrepreneurs hire Copy Writers for assistance with web pages, sales letters, advertising, books, etc. Your minimum cash outlay is probably one of the lowest. Factor in the cost of your computer, electricity and cable, let's say $50 for the month, and that is your start-up cost. Now let's say you charge a flat fee of $2,500 for helping your customer write 5 sales pages. You're actual labor cost is $450, plus your monthly

cost of $50, and you have $500 into the job. You've made a $2,000 profit! Not bad for a few hours of work. But make sure that you finish your job on a timely basis and that you have not stolen copy from another source. If those things happen, your client may ask for a refund, or ask you to redo the job properly. This will all be lost money.

3) **Envelope Stuffing** – Ever see those ads for stuffing envelopes? Yes, they are real jobs. But before taking on the job make sure that it is legitimate. You don't want to get in trouble for an illegal mailing list. The start-up cost is generally $0.00 if the client is supplying the letters, envelopes and stamps. If not, the cost per each unit would be around $.50, which would be billed back to the client with your fee. Now let's say that the client is paying you $.25 per unit, and you have 1,000 envelopes to stuff. That's $250 in your pocket, with ZERO cash outlay. Not bad for a day's work.

4) Home –Based Daycare – Whether you have a young child at home that you are taking care of, or the children are all in school, or an "empty nest", having child care out of your home is a great way to earn extra money. Your start-up costs might be a little higher, depending on the cost of your license, and supplies needed. Depending on the number and the ages of the children you will be watching, the first thing you will need to do is make sure that the house and surrounding area are safe. You will need a fenced in yard, rails and gates on porches, fire extinguishers and fire alarms, repairs to wooden decks, etc. You will also need to have enough supplies to properly take care of them. For example: crib(s), diapers, toys for inside and outside, extra clothes, safety items (plugs for outlets, toilet clamps, drawer and cabinet locks), first aid kit, learning toys, jungle gym or swing set, snacks, breakfast, lunch & possibly dinner food, etc. Your initial investment plus monthly expenses breaks down to $1,200 a month. You charge $250/week per child, and you are allowed to care for 6 children a week. That's $1,500 per week, or $6,000 per month. You've paid for your initial investment the first week of your business.

As you can see, it's very easy to figure out if a business will be worth your time and investment. Granted, there will always be hidden costs that come up, but if properly budgeted from the beginning, chances are that your business will start to make money almost immediately.

Another way to make this process more realistic is to go to **www.members.mcbov.info,** go to the *Business Management Database* section and play around with the worksheets provided online, specifically the spreadsheets titled "Sales Forecast for Twelve Months," "Business Plan," and so on. They are all available for your analysis.

Last but not least, go online to commonly used search engines. Look for frequently searched key word terms, and pick the ones with the most monthly inquiries.

Chapter 3

Establishing A Business Presence

How do you know if it's best to start a business alone or with another person? The first step is to consult a lawyer. Your lawyer will help you decide which form of business entity will be the best fit for you and your business.

There are many different types, so let's look at the breakdown of each business entity:

- **Sole Proprietorship:** A Sole Proprietorship is owned and run by one individual, and there is no legal distinction between the owner and the business. Even though the owner collects all profits, he/she is also liable for all business debts and income/loss from the business. The most common reason entrepreneurs start businesses this way is because they are easy to organize, and require a small amount of start-up capital.
- **General Partnership:** In a General Partnership, each of the two or more partners will equally share in both the liability and the responsibility of the company. The income and expense is reported on a separate return for tax purposes, but each partner then reports his or her pro-rata share of the profit or loss from the business as one line on his personal tax return.
- **Limited Partnership:** With a limited partnership, each of the general partners has unlimited liability for the debts of the partnership, but the limited partner's exposure to the debts of the partnership is limited to the contribution each has made to the partnership. With certain minor exceptions, the reporting for tax purposes is the same as for a general partnership.
- **Corporation:** A Corporation, or a "C Corp", is an independent legal entity owned by shareholders. A Corporation allows two

or more investors limited liability, meaning that they are not obligated for the debts of the corporation, and that creditors can look only to the corporation's assets for payment. In this type of entity, the investors are obligated to file their own tax returns and pay taxes on their personal income. Corporations are generally recommended for larger businesses that have a high number of employees. They also tend to have a complicated legal and tax obligation, as well as costly administrative fees. But a Corporation also has great tax benefits, such as deductibility of health insurance premiums.

- **"S" Corporation:** An "S" Corporation is treated as a partnership for tax purposes, while it is also treated as a regular corporation for other purposes. Profits and losses from the business can be passed through to your personal tax return. This option has great tax benefits for someone just starting out who wants to keep costs low.
- **Limited Liability:** A Limited Liability Company (LLC) provides limited liability for all of its members, but typically can be treated as a partnership for federal income tax purposes. In an LLC, one partner is not responsible or liable for another partner's misconduct or negligence. State laws may differ as to whether it is treated as a partnership or a corporation for state income tax purposes. It can be managed by all of the members or can have centralized management in one or more of the members.

For details on all options available for federal income tax purposes, or to learn more about setting up company entities, visit **www.mcbov.info.**

Location, Location, Location

In order to establish a business presence I expect that you have chosen a suitable business, researched all aspects of it, and are now prepared with a feasible start-up cost budget. But will you be working from home, or do you need to work outside of the house and have a storefront location? Let's break each one down:

> **Home Based Business:** The typical thing to do is to get a business mailing address (P.O. Box or virtual office if you're running the business from home) a local or toll-free number with voicemail, and a business tax ID.

> **Storefront Location:** Here you may use the actual address of the location, plus you will also require a local or toll-free number with voicemail, and a business tax ID. You may also want to have 1 or more staff members to help with reception, phones, and customers.

If you are not sure which situation will be best for you and your business, then save yourself the hassle of doing everything yourself, and take the easier way out by hiring a professional. I will be happy to assist you with your needs. Just call me at (888) 948-3247 for a free consultation.

Business Resources

One of the worst things a business owner can do is to resist or overlook compliances with licensing and permit requirements. By doing so this could result in additional fees and penalty payments. So no matter what you think of the licensing process, don't neglect it, or you may regret it! I recommend you register it properly. For instance, if you're looking forward to establishing a business in a different state than where you live, most states require a registered agent with an address presence. Please go directly to **www.reviews.mcbov.info** for additional information.

The most cost-effective way to register your business with the State of Illinois is via mail; that is, if you are not in a hurry to start, because it can take six to eight weeks to process. This step is not mandatory if you're just starting out with a website that just sells information. However, if the type of business you choose requires state licensing like insurance or real estate, then state registration is required. It is very convenience to do it online if you are willing to pay a little more money.

The filing fees vary from state to state. For example, it is much cheaper to file an LLC in Missouri than it is in Illinois. It depends on where you feel comfortable conducting business. My first LLC was formed online in Missouri for only $50, plus a registered agent for $99 per year.

Obtaining a tax ID is optional when starting a business, but I strongly recommend it in order to keep better track of business operations and earnings, for establishing a business bank account, and for obtaining business credit cards and loan approvals. Get yours free at **www.reviews.mcbov.info.**

Last but not least, register a Business Credit Profile. The main reason to consider opening this type of profile is to build business (corporate) credit because depending on the type of business you decide to go with, most suppliers will check your business credit profile to determine your eligibility for credit. Unfortunately, the most common reason many companies would report your credit is if they have something bad to say about you or your business performance. To get started on the right path, it'll be a good idea to do business with suppliers who will help build your credit profile. Some of them can be located on my website at **mcbov.info.**

Get your business a credit profile right at the beginning rather than later. One thing you have to understand with credit bureaus like D&B

(Dun & Bradstreet) is that you need to use a physical address, rather than a P.O. Box, and have a local or toll-free phone number, not a cell phone. Another reason to get started sooner than later is the fact you get to separate your personal credit from business credit, and the same goes for establishing a separate business bank account and business credit cards.

"Sometimes when you innovate, you make mistakes. It is best to admit them quickly, and get on with improving your other innovations."

~Steve Jobs~

Chapter 4

Playing the Name Game

Playing the Name Game

By now you should have a business name in mind. Choosing your business name is as important as choosing your business, if not more so. The important fact to remember is to pick a name that totally epitomizes your brand identity. Example: If you own a carpet cleaning business you wouldn't name your company "We Can Help You." What does this name tell anyone about you or your business? Nothing. Now try "Carpets Clean and Bright." Now everyone knows exactly what your business is.

The first name you fall in love with can be a major disaster. But believe it or not, many business owners will become obstinate and won't let go. To them, it's become a part of their "Big Dream."

Now just by following a few simple rules, you'll be able to put that stubbornness on the side and open your eyes and mind to other enhanced possibilities:

- **Keep it short and simple**. Your name should not only be easy to remember, but also easy to pronounce.

- **Avoid foreign names**. I understand that you are proud of your heritage, and you want to honor the family by calling your business "Ricciardiello Bookkeeping," but will people really know how to spell it when they are looking for you?

- **Avoid acronyms or initials**. Is being the first name in the directory your major goal with your name? The "ABCCo" might seem like the perfect solution, but it fails to tell people who you are and what your business does. And besides, there are plenty of businesses out there that start with 'A', "AA", or "AAA." Don't you want to stand out from the crowd? And as far as alphabetical combinations are concerned, would people really remember "CDFZ Marine Retailers"?

- **Avoid names that can be pronounced more than one way.** It's never a good sign when people are looking at your name and trying to figure out what it means: "Codfish Marine Retailers" "CeeDeeFizzy Marine Retailers." Get the point?

- **Avoid using words that can have more than one meaning.** Unless this is your 50th company and you are purposefully trying to go for tongue-in-cheek, be careful of the one word that could have multiple meanings… ex. "Peters Poop Deck." It just might be offensive to others.

- **Avoid multiple words in a name.** For example, if you name your business "Thingamabob Business Services," think about how your website domain would end up: "thingamabobbusinessservices.com." The double "b's" and triple "S's" are sure to do more than confuse perspective customers.

When all else fails, keep this in mind: when you are choosing a name for your product or business:

a. Decide what you want your name **to do** for your business or product.
b. What does your name say about your company?
c. What does your name say about your product?
d. Is your name catchy and easy to understand?
e. Is your name memorable?

Namestorming

How do you create great names? Are there rules and guidelines for that, too? Let's look at the subhead above. We used a technique by way of combining two words together to create a new, descriptive word:

"name" + "brainstorming" = "namestorming"

It's very easy for you to do that for your business, too. All you need to do is to pick two words that represent your company and what it does: For example, let's take a look at the word "Travelocity." Broken down, this equals "travel" + "velocity." Broken down a little more and it indicates speedy and effective travel.

I know I previously stated to avoid using acronyms, but there can be exceptions to this rule. Have you ever heard of the company *American Family Life Assurance Company?* Of course you have. It's none other than ...AFLAC! You may not remember its exact name, but when you hear "AFLAC" you think of a ducks' quack, which make you think of the AFLAC duck, therefore the insurance company. Brilliant branding campaign!

So if you do it properly and have an awesome branding promotion that will clearly cement an image in people's minds, then using an acronym that not only makes sense as a word, but brings an instant mental picture, can and will work.

Now think about which of these methods are most relevant when you are deciding on your business or product name:

- Using descriptive words

- Using a nonsense word that is fun and catchy
- Using a relevant symbol that triggers association
- Using your name, or a combination of yours and your partner's
- Using two words combined
- Using a word that triggers a visual image

Once you have decided on your business name, you will need to check if not only the name itself is available, but also your domain name. There's nothing worse than picking a great name and finding out someone already has a website with that name. Ouch!

Also, be sure to properly register your business name. For more information on what you need to do, visit **http://www.sba.gov.**

Chapter 5

Focusing On Your Branding

Focusing On Your Branding

Whether or not you are branding your product name or your business name, your strategy should hit these four targets:

1. **Consistency:** This is the key element. Look at McDonalds. Why has it been so successful for over 50 years? Because it has been *consistent* over all these years. You know what to expect when you order a Big Mac ... Two all beef patties, special sauce, lettuce, cheese, pickles, onions on a sesame seed bun. It's always been, and always will be, because it works.

2. **Acceptance:** Your branding campaign, especially your first one, needs to draw your customers in. *"Two all beef patties, special sauce, lettuce, cheese, pickles, onions on a sesame seed bun."* You've heard it a million times, and that is what you first think of when you hear "Big Mac."

3. **Familiarity**: If you have created your brand consistency and customer acceptance, then this will happen almost naturally. Just think of FedEx – *"When it absolutely, positively has to be there on time."*

4. **Unique Edge:** To capture not only your customer's attention, but your competitors' market share, a unique edge is absolutely crucial. You need:

    - To solve a problem that similar products haven't
    - To make sure it works better than your competitors' does
    - Your product priced comparably
    - A dynamic look to the product

- Unique bonuses
- An extraordinary Customer Service Center

Keep in mind that you should find that these elements will be so much easier to put in place once you are able to clearly identify your market.

Your Branding Success

If you want to know the difference between the Goliaths and the Lilliputians, you'll find that the Goliaths will spend millions on *pre-testing*. Just take a look at Hollywood directors. They don't just make a movie and immediately put it out for the world to see. They pre-test their movie with focus groups. They see how the public reacts to a particular character or scene, which ending they prefer, the flow of the story, etc. Once they have these items ironed out, then and only then will they release their movie.

Another step to do is to re-examine the results at different times to be sure that they are still on target. Focus on:

- **Pre-release:** Test your product's name, attractiveness, functionality, etc. along with your branding strategy on a closed, limited-run number of your target audience. For participating, give away a special offer to an affiliate or forum member, or a free bonus to the first X-number of people who sign up for your newsletter.
- **Post-launch:** This will show you if you are on target with your predictions and expectations – or not.

Although analyses should be going on at all times behind the scenes, it's up to you to decide when you will officially test and re-measure your branding metrics. No matter how wildly successful you are at launch point, if you don't adopt this process, it is inevitable that you will be sabotaged by that absolute enemy of testing... assumption. And assumptions always lose you money.

We've already discussed how important consistency is to your brand success. Once those initial tests have shown public acceptance and there are no more bugs to be ironed out, consistency has to be maintained.

Be sure to put serious thought into the following when you are in your initial planning stages:

- How are you going to maintain consistency?
- Which parts of your business should stay consistent, and where should you plan for growth and expansion?
- Which elements in your product should always be consistent, and which can change without negatively affecting sales?
- Which elements do your target markets want to keep the same?

When you have followed these procedures and all of these elements are in place, then and only then will you begin to build true brand familiarity.

Refining Your Strategies

Here are some strategies, many of them free, that you can easily use to create your initial branding campaign:

- Article marketing
- Blogging
- Charity sponsorship
- Contests

- Direct marketing (postcards, flyers)
- Email campaigns
- Physical, local public events
- Pinterest Pinboards
- Polls
- PPC advertising
- Samples
- Social networking integration
- Webinars
- YouTube videos

Focus on which of these strategies brings in the most recognition and return, while paying attention to your ROI (Return On Investment).

One final tip: Always be sure to combine both **inspiration and process** in your business, and you'll be well on the road to business branding success.

Chapter 6

Building A Business Plan

Building A Business Plan

After selecting a business specialty and working on your brand, what's your next step? You need to lay the groundwork of a successful business, and you cannot do that without a thorough analysis of your business and the marketplace in which you want to succeed.

Here you will want to put together a business plan. A business plan is like an architectural blueprint or resume. You can do this on your own or hire a professional. A good business plan will center on reachable goals and projected targets. Goals and targets may be related to income, the number of units sold, market shares, profit margins, or any other measurement. They may be monthly, quarterly or annual goals.

A business plan is a work in progress. There are companies that make business planning an ongoing activity, because business planning is most effective when it is done frequently and consistently. The process of reviewing progress on business goals and targets, while also setting new ones, should take place monthly, weekly, and daily.

Meeting Goals and Targets

Your main components should include the following:

- **Current Balance Sheet** - A financial statement that is used to calculate the net worth of a business. This statement will list all of the assets, liabilities and equity of a company at a specific point in time – quarterly, bi-yearly, yearly.
- **Pro Forma Balance Sheet** – This is a financial statement where the data reflected is on an 'as if' basis. For example, if a company was considering purchasing another company, they would prepare a "pro forma financial statement" to estimate what effect the purchase would have on its own financial condition.

- **Income Statement** - Your financial statement that measures your company's financial performance, including net profit and loss, over a specific accounting period, like a fiscal quarter or year.
- **Cash Flow Analysis** – This is often used for financial reporting purposes. This analysis shows a company's receipts and expenses during a specific period.

The balance sheet measures assets (any item of economic value) vs. liabilities (legal debt or obligation) which should be equal, or "balanced;" the income statement measures how much money your business earns in a quarter or a year; and the cash flow analysis measures how much cash comes in and out of your business. These measurements, and others, will help you handle your resources more effectively in order to make prudent business decisions. They also provide precise information about your company, its strengths, its weaknesses, and its contingency plans.

Business Funding Section

If your business requires funding from banks and private lenders, often it will be based on a well-written, articulated business plan. The first components of a business plan consist of a cover sheet, a statement of purpose, and a table of contents. In addition, it must state the type of business, such as the description of marketing (the process of communicating the value of a product or service to customers), a competitive advantage (an advantage that a firm has over its competitors), and an operation process (manner of functioning or operating). The type of business insurance, the financial records, and the loan applications are also important factors, as long as they relate to your choice of business. Others to implement are a break-even analysis, a *pro forma* income projection (the potential financial position of a company), a three-year summary detail (monthly, quarterly, yearly), and *pro forma* cash flow (projected statement of cash flow). If this is too confusing to handle, just have it done professionally.

To get a business loan or access to credit, your business needs a positive track record. Generally, in order to get significant funding a company must be in business for at least six months, or for larger loans or lines of credit you must be in business for two to three years. You will also need a good personal credit rating.

When starting a business from home, depending on the type of business, you need to consider how your products are produced and from where they will be shipped. Consider entering into a partnership with a web-based company such as Amazon or eBay that will fulfill the orders and ship the products on your behalf. The costs for such services will differ from what you would pay to do it yourself, so be sure to figure in these costs in your business plan.

Furthermore, depending on the type of business, other components to consider are your supporting documents, such as your tax returns of principals for the last three years and a personal financial statement. For a franchised business, make sure to have a copy of your contract, provided by the franchiser. Provide copies of the proposed lease or purchase agreement for building space, for licenses and other legal documents, including but not limited to letters of intent from your potential suppliers.

Short Business Plan Example

I know this all sounds confusing to you, but it can be really simple. Let's break this down into easy layman's terms:

Business Description

- **Who We Are:** We are ABC Cleaning Company. We offer

affordable cleaning services so that our clients can live better quality lives. We are established providers with experienced and insured contractors.

- **The type of business you offer**: We provide housekeeping services to local residences via monthly contracts.
- **Supply & Demand:** The demand for such services outweighs supplies based on recent surveys/research. Due to this shortage for such services, our company's position has great potential for stable growth.
- **SWOT Analysis:** (Strengths, Weaknesses, Opportunities, and Threats) We have a low overhead cost since the business is operated out of the home. Our contractors provide their own insurance and are paid per job performed, unlike most competitors who hire employees who are paid per hour. Our opportunities are vast and our competition few (including major companies).

Internet & Market Description

- **Presence:** The type of housekeeping services we provide is founded on quality and prompt performance. Our presence is recognizable and appreciated in our community.
- **Purpose:** The purpose of our business is to cater to both residential homes and commercial office cleaning needs in the community and surrounding areas.
- **Business Model:** All of our accounts are acquired via contract bids (3 month-12 month memberships).

Company Products

- **Product A:** Residential Cleaning, basic and advanced housekeeping

- **Product B:** Commercial Cleaning, basic and advance maintenance

<u>Funding</u>

- **Amount Needed**: $1,000-$2,500
- **Funding History:** Owners Equity, friends, and family
- **Reason for Loan:** To purchase additional vacuum cleaners, buffer, and general cleaning supplies

<u>Marketing</u>

- We plan to utilize several marketing methods, including Direct Mail, Sales Contractors, email, Telephone, online Ads, and Newspaper Ads.

<u>Projections/Expectations</u>

- **Revenue:** $3,500-$5,000/month for the next 3-5 years
- **Cost of Sales:** 20% of revenue
- **Gross Profit:** 80% of revenue
- **Operating Expenses:** 15% of revenue
- **New Income:** $2,275-$3,250

If you feel that this might be out of your comfort zone, then contact us at **www.consulting.mcbov.info** for our start-up consulting package, which includes a company business plan.

We also have several pre-formulated business plan spreadsheets available on our website. Under "Business Database," scroll-down the page to locate the link to the "Business Plan" and fill in the blanks.

"There are no secrets to success. It is the result of preparation, hard work, and learning from failure."

~Colin Powell~

Chapter 7

Incorporating Your Vision Statement and Mission Objectives

Now that the company is set up and financially secure (for the moment) let's talk about where you see your business going. The following items have helped me tremendously. The purpose is to get you engaged in your business idea until the "who," "what," "when," "where," and "how" components of your potential business entity are absolutely black and white in your mind. Once you have a clear picture, it will help you get additional funding and support.

Your Vision Statement and Mission Objectives

Vision statement: *A picture of the future ("where we are headed") that we seek to create, such as a dream or a general idea.*

A vision statement is one sentence or a short paragraph that includes a broad, inspirational image of the future. Vision statements, therefore, contain details of the future direction of your enterprise (the future plans with aims and objectives). These types of statements will focus on tomorrow.

A mission Objective: *Your purpose or reason for existing. For example, the "who" and "what" the business is about. It is the vehicle for reaching the vision.*

A mission statement is a sentence or short paragraph written to reflect a company's core purpose, identity, values, and principal business aims. Mission statements, therefore, contain important information about a company. In a nutshell, this should include the company's mission (what the company does, its products, its services, and its customers).

You might ask, "How long should a vision statement be?" Well, a good statement is a sentence or short paragraph consisting of two to four sentences.

Learning how to write a vision statement takes time! It needs to be positive and inspirational. Take your time when writing a vision statement. It's a hard but very important task. You will almost certainly have to revise it many times before you're happy with it.

For instance, your vision and mission statement can look like the following example:

Advance Auto Parts Inc. Mission Statement

"It is the mission of Advance Auto Parts to provide personal vehicle owners and enthusiasts with the vehicle related products and knowledge that fulfill their wants and needs at the right price. Our friendly, knowledgeable and professional staff will help inspire, educate and problem-solve for our customers."

Piecing Together Your Business Model

The business model dates back to the earliest days of business. It describes the way in which a company generates revenue or makes money. A business model can be simple or very complex. A restaurant's business model is to make money by cooking and serving food to hungry customers. A website's business model might not be as clear, as there are many ways in which these types of companies can generate revenue. For example, some make money by providing free services and then selling advertising to other companies, while others might sell a product or service directly to online customers. One more example is when companies require a membership fee to join and participate in their services. This is one of the easiest examples to show what a business model looks like. This type of company generates a majority of its revenue or profit from selling memberships.

You need to decide what product or service you are going to offer, and how you can produce a profit by engaging in this activity. There are certain questions that you need to ask yourself, and here we will take a look at them in short detail:

1) **What is your strategy for operations, sales, marketing?**

   Once you decide on your basic business model, you need to figure out how to make it work in real life. A strategic plan entails the "how we will get there" blueprint. A company founded on a well-outlined strategy will have positioned itself to have a competitive advantage. This is crucial to set up right at the beginning of developing your business. It doesn't matter if your business is perceived to be small at first because as long as you figure out how to make the business profitable and successful, it will only become logical to expand and grow or sell it to a bigger company.

2) **Why will this business succeed?**

   Ask yourself some important questions, and answer them honestly. Is there a market for your product or service? Who is your typical customer? Who are your competitors? For you to succeed there must be a clear *demand* for your product or service. This can be hard to determine at the beginning, but if you can already see it as a success in great detail, chances are you will make it happen at all costs. My advice is to write every thought down on paper and keep a record. The best way to answer it is to do a market test or study product trends. More specifically, develop a prototype or a sample of your product and put it up for sale at any merchant sites like eBay or Amazon to see how it does.

3) **Why is this product or service useful?**

   This is the first thing an entrepreneur needs to figure out. The more you can figure out the need and usefulness of your particular product or service, the higher your chances are to succeed profitably. How will your product or service make people's lives better, or solve a problem for them?

4) **What will the product do for the user?**

Every product or service offered should have a benefit to society. In essence, you should clarify the benefits for the end user of your product. Also, state what sets your product or service apart from your competitors' products or services.

5) **What is the expected life cycle of the product?**

Are you selling a product that may go out of style, like trendy clothing? Can it be superseded by new technology? Any perishable product must show its expiration date, and any consumer product must have an expected service life. As for services, state how long services are good for per fee.

6) **How do technology advances affect your products or services?**

We live in a time when technology advances affect everything we do, for the most part, and acknowledging its effects on your products or services can save your business in the long run, and prepare you for future competitive advantage opportunities. Other important issues relating to this subject are product liability, uniqueness, and the ability to meet customer needs.

7) **Does the product have brand-name recognition?**

This is the case where you select a business with previous existence and is well recognized by the public. If you are looking to start a home-based business then it will have to be created from scratch, unless you join a network marketing company with a recognized brand, like Amway or Avon. A brand name goes beyond the product or services offered. If you're looking to build a business that will last forever, then consider the customer experience and stakeholders' expectations. Be sure to learn from the best companies who have managed to accomplish great brand images, and develop one that fits your goals and strategy.

8) **Are there repeat uses for the product?**

This is an important question! Frequent usage is a great feature to incorporate in product development, because once you have the ability to get a customer hooked, it's an indicator for long-term business sustainability and profitability of a company. It's a good measure of customer satisfaction and retention, and with a product that can be purchased over and over again (like food or personal care products) you can develop a core base of consumers who will become loyal to your product. Is the consumer the end user of the product?

The "end user" is defined as the person who uses a product or service. I strongly advise you to consider this when developing a product because at the end of the day, their satisfaction is one of the determinants of your success.

9) **Is this a high quality or low-quality product?**

Quality can be described as products or services built with superior vs. inferior materials or a combination of the two, with a majority of materials being of exceptional service. You may choose to compete in the marketplace on the basis of *price*, where you are offering an inexpensive product or service; or you may choose to compete on the basis of *quality*, where you charge a premium price but you deliver exceptional quality.

10) Are there any substitutes for your product?

A substitute is defined as goods that can be used to satisfy the same needs or as a replacement. If there are substitutes for your products or services, then figure out how to differentiate yourself and clearly define what sets you apart from the rest. This is harder to do than it seems, therefore a detailed and well-researched business plan will save you time and money.

Let's look at an example of product substitutions:

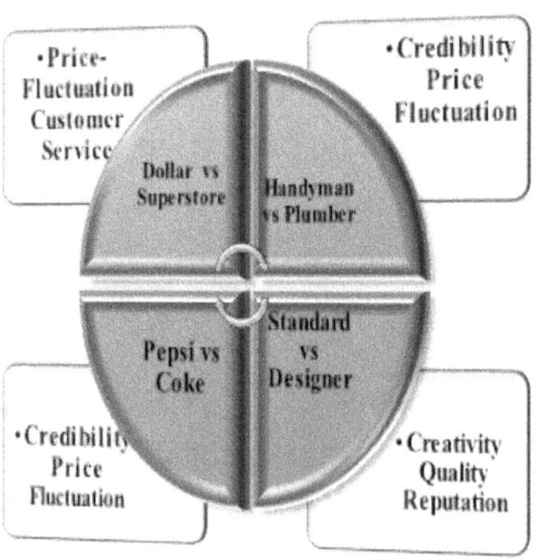

As you can see, the diagram above is divided into four quadrants. Each of the quadrants includes two products or services that may seem similar: Dollar vs. Superstore, Handyman vs. Plumber, Standard vs. Designer, and Pepsi vs. Coke. Yet each of the four pairs can be differentiated on the basis of credibility, price, reputation, quality, or customer service.

How will your product or service stand out from your competitors?

Chapter 8

Budgeting Your Business

The one part of having a business that scares everyone is the budget. It scares me, too! Seeing in black and white how much money you need to make every month to pay your outgoing debts, and seeing how much, or little, is left at the end of the month is a daunting process. But having a business budget will help you boost your chances of success, and (hopefully) reduce your levels of stress.

Let's take a look at the basics that you will need to focus on:

1. **Start-up**
   This is the amount of capital (money) that you have to invest in your business at the beginning.
2. **Projected income**
   This is the amount of money that you feel you can make weekly, monthly, quarterly and yearly.
3. **Operating costs**
   These are the expenses that you have every month to operate your business: supplies, advertising, marketing, etc.

When you have a solid indication of your budget, then and only then can you start to make educated decisions about your spending.

One thing most entrepreneurs forget to add into their budget is their own salary. The majority of the experts I have spoken with agree that first and foremost you need to pay yourself. Now you can turn around and put your paycheck back into the business if need be, but it is always best to show that you yourself are making money, as well as your business.

The next step in the process is to determine your potential costs, or expenses. There are many programs available to help with this process, including my own pre-formulated calculation spreadsheet:

Start-up Expenses	
Company Name	This is where you put your company name.
Property Ownership ✓ Purchase ✓ Construction ✓ Remodeling ✓ Total	For a Home-Based Business – Space to be used in your property still counts.
Leasehold Improvements ✓ Asset 1 ✓ Asset 2 Total Leaseholds	Assets that can be depreciated over time by a landlord.
Capital Equipment ✓ Furniture ✓ Equipment ✓ Fixtures Total Capital Equipment	Capital Equipment is used to manufacture your product or service.

The next diagram/table provides a brief explanation of the different subjects and components involved in a start-up analysis and process. This may seem overwhelming at first, but if you push yourself to get through it a couple of times you will come to learn its effectiveness.

Sources of Capital

Sources of Capital ✓ Bank Loans ✓ Personal ✓ Grants ✓ Savings ✓ Stock Investors ✓ Owner(s)'s ✓	This is where you plan to get funds for your business. It could be from one or multiple sources.

Investment Total Sources of Capital	
Collateral For Loans ✓ Real Estate ✓ Paper Assets ✓ Goods/Products Total Value	This is the area where you have to figure out how you're able to provide security for money you plan to borrow.
Business Owners ✓ Your Name Here ✓ Other Owner ✓ Other Owner	This section is basically where you state the parties involved who are going to be part of your business entity.
Loan Guarantors ✓ Guarantor 1 ✓ Guarantor 2	This is an important factor for securing a loan in case of default.

I use this quite often whenever I have a new business idea I'd like to test. It really makes a difference to put all your ideas on paper and determine the feasibility or validity of an idea based on the real-life calculations.

Your Budget

As a new business owner, some of the things that you will need to budget for include:

- *Autoresponder
- Office Supplies
- Computer
- Travel
- Business Coach or Mentor

- Promotional Materials
- Office Equipment
- Advertising
- Domain Registration
- Vehicle Maintenance
- Staff
- Internet Service
- Telephone Service
- Online Fees
- Web Hosting Fees
- Antivirus Program

*Top quality Autoresponders such as Aweber or GetResponse are very affordable at less than $20 a month.

Some of the above items you may already have (e.g. vehicle, computer), while others you will need to budget for a continuous monthly basis, and still others will need to be purchased only once.

Support is Key

The more research you do on your business ideas, the more exact your projected costs will be. One way to figure this out is to temporarily work for an employer within your business choice to learn everything you can about the typical costs associated with your preferred business. If you are not too thrilled with becoming a spy, the most logical option is to just ask around. Talk to successful entrepreneurs, managers, and business owners in that particular field of interest. I also recommend reading business books, listening to audios, and attending live events. Surprisingly, you can learn valuable information and form important partnerships.

Regardless of which option you decided to go with, the next action is mandatory, and that is to join a club or society of like minds, desires, and vision. A good example of this is if you want to become a realtor. You would join a club or become part of the association of realtors. Many rich and wealthy Americans belong to a particular club, professional association, or support group to help them along the way.

Business associations that you can consider joining include your local Chamber of Commerce, the Rotary Club, the Black Business Association, American Business Women's Association, and many more.

Having a solid support group around you is very important. Have you wondered why some people win the lotto and in the next year or two they are bankrupt? Or have you tried very hard to become successful running your own business online or from home, and it seems that you are never getting anywhere and are left with only frustration, discouragement, and a sense of wasted time? If you decide to walk alone on the path to wealth and success, then you may find the way to be very difficult. Now there are always exceptions to the rules, and you might prove me wrong. But for the vast majority of entrepreneurs, three things will set you on the right path to success in business: recognizing your weaknesses and strengths, asking for help, and being willing to do whatever it takes to make your business prosper profitably.

"There is only one boss: The Customer. And he can fire everybody in the company from the chairman on down, simply by spending his money somewhere else."

~Sam Walton~

Chapter 9

Building The Foundation Of Your Business

You have the major criteria for your business already in place. You have your company name, your home office, your business license, your budget and your goals for your company.

So what's next?

Now is the time to start building the foundation of your business: your web site. It doesn't matter if you're just starting out, or already have an established business and want to expand. One of the most important parts of your business is having a website that will draw new clients into your circle.

Think of your web site as the primary connection between you and your customers. As much time as you put in creating your company, you need to put in as much time, or more, into your website. Research has shown that it takes between 3-5 seconds for a perspective client to make up his mind about whether or not he will do business with you, just based on your website. First impressions matter big time.

Your website is the storefront of your business. It is the display case not only for your company, but for your products and services. A poorly designed website will turn customers away just as a poorly designed store will. But with a store, a customer might not want to get in their car and go elsewhere. They might spend more time looking for what they want because of the convenience of already being there. But on the internet, moving on to another location is done by the click of a button.

How to Choose a Domain Name

Before you are ready to choose a domain name, go to the Google Key Word Tool at **www.googlekeywordtool.com.** Put in the name of the type of business you are interested in inside the search box, and then press "submit." Next you want to look for the key words that have the most traffic, such as 500,000 people searching locally or higher.

Why go through all this trouble? Simple: choosing a business name or domain name that not enough people are searching for online will only hurt your traffic and sales potential. However, with the right business name, you are going to be a traffic magnet, attracting from five hundred to five thousand visitors to your site on a monthly basis. I've made the mistake of bypassing this step in the past, and it has cost me plenty.

Naming Your Domain

Your domain name is generally the first thing people learn about your company. This is usually found through search engine results, word of mouth, or advertising. So be sure to give your domain name careful attention before you register it. Customers want to remember your name, and if it is easy enough, they are more likely to visit your site first. So be sure that your name is easy to spell, easy to remember, and use as few characters as possible. You want to get your customers to your site fast. No one wants to remember if a domain name is www.Carpets-Fresh-and-Clean.com

or

www.Carpets_Fresh_and_Clean.com.

Way too confusing.

By far the best domain name to use is the actual name of your company, as in *www.carpetsfreshandclean.com.* However, if you've found that that name is already taken by someone else in another state, then it would be appropriate to put in the break characters. Or put your name first, as in *www.michelescarpetsfreshandclean.com*, or even shorten the name to *www.cleancarpets.com*. I think you get the idea. Just try to be sure that your actual business name and your website name correlate.

The most popular thing right now is to buy previously used domain names in order to redirect that traffic to your website. It's brilliant, really, because it saves you time, hassle, and money in the long run, except that sometimes it can be costly. Note: If you decide to go this route, be sure that if you can't get the exact name you want, get as close as possible.

You can register your domain name through any number of companies that provide domain name reservations. Most of these are free services. However, it will save you a step—and possibly some trouble—if you register directly through the web site host you plan to use.

Selecting a Web Host

There are thousands of web hosting companies to choose from, so be sure to pick the one that will be right for your business. As with anything else, it is always a good idea to research web host companies before signing on with one.

Before selecting your web host, consider some of the following:

- **Discounts and Contracts:** There are many web hosts that will provide service without a contract, as well as those who require that you sign a contract with them. This could be for 12 or 24 months, or it could be on a month-to-month basis. In addition, for customers who pay for multiple months up front, the web hosts might be inclined to offer a discount, or maybe even offer a bundle package.

- **Free e-mail address:** There are web hosting services that will provide you with e-mail addresses that match your domain name, such as **you@yourdomain.com.**
- **Bandwidth:** Bandwidth is the amount of information that can be sent over a network connection in a given period of time. Even though this isn't as much of a problem as it was in the past, be sure that your web host provides enough bandwidth to keep your web site up and running smoothly.
- **Expandability:** As your business grows, so should your web site. A competent web host will suggest upgrading your hosting package to include more storage, bandwidth and additional features as needed.
- **Storage space:** As you need plenty of closet space for your shoes, your files also need a sufficient amount of storage space.
- **Technical Support and Customer Service:** Technical support will definitely be needed when you least expect it, so be sure that there is a phone number listed on their website, and that they are available 24/7, either through live chat or by phone.
- **Design options:** Many of the web hosts will offer easy-to-use drag-and-drop design programs or customizable page templates for site building. Templates are an easy way to create professional-looking web sites.

The Whole Enchilada

When trying to creating the most professional environment, there are two main elements to consider:

1. a visually appealing site, and
2. understanding the way it reads.

- **Design.** You have only three seconds to capture the attention of your visitors, so this is why your web sites' appearance is so critical. But you have to have the right balance: too flashy will not only take longer to load, it will also turn many prospects off, and too plain will put them to sleep. So when you are designing your web site, try to attain a natural balance between words and images that will not only provide the correct visual attraction, but that will quickly load.

  Navigation is also important when designing your website. Your visitors want to find their information quickly, so they need to move effortlessly from sector to sector. Use floating drop boxes and side bars, along with links on each page to your contact page, ordering page, and home page.

- **Web copy.** Once you have your fabulous design, you are ready for your professional copy. Now I'm not saying that you have to have a professional write it for you, but sometimes it is a lot easier. But if you are going to write the content yourself, pay strict attention to your grammar, spelling, font styles, colors, sizes, and your written word. What do I mean by this? Most magazine articles and newspapers use the sixth-grade reading level. Now, I am not saying that people are stupid or illiterate, but the quicker they understand what you are saying, the happier they are and are more likely to place an order.

Just keep in mind that your web copy needs to be informative, free of advertising propaganda, carefully crafted, and most importantly, targeted to your business.

Chapter 10

The Power of Marketing

In today's savvy world, it's just not enough to have an excellent business idea or product. You need to market it! So what is marketing? Marketing is the method used to decide what products may be of interest to customers and the strategy to use in getting the word out. It also contributes to the strategy that formulates sales techniques, business communication, and business developments. In the end, it helps companies form strong customer relationships and brand/image building.

To get the most out of your marketing you will not only need to invest your time and energy, but also your cash and resources. Your approach will depend not only on how much of each you currently have, but you will also need to be adaptable as you adjust your campaigns.

Marketing is used to identify the customer, satisfy the customer, and keep the customer. With the customer as the focus of its activities, marketing management is a major factor of business management. It evolved to meet the immobility in developing new markets caused by mature market's overcrowding in the last few centuries. The adoption of marketing strategies requires businesses to shift their focus from the perceived needs and wants of their customers in order to boost profitability.

Keep this in mind: there is only one marketing mistake that you can make, and that would be if you were to "wing it." Having a marketing plan set up in advance will give you a solid foundation on which to build your business.

The Marketing Plan

If your Business Plan is the "heads" side of a coin, then your Marketing Plan would be the "tails." Think of how many great opportunities you would miss out on to grow your business with a one sided coin.

Your marketing plan should anticipate the needs and wants of future customers, while necessitating the process for achieving your company's goals. One of the best ways to market your business is on the Internet. Get listed on the most popular search engines; some merchants use a site submitter, which can save you time by sending your site to as many as one thousand search engines.

The following steps are strongly recommended for low start-up budgets because they're very cost effective and user friendly. The most popular merchant sites are auction sites at auctionsites.com; Craig's List at craigslist.org; Amazon at amazon.com; Click Bank at clickbank.com. The beauty of posting your products on these sites is that your product is guaranteed to be exposed to thousands, even millions, of shoppers. Have you ever searched for a product on a search engine and come to find it appearing at the top of the first page results, comparing two or three market place prices? Well, normally you'll see Amazon as one of them, as long as a vendor is selling that particular product on that site. It's the same with Craigslist. When you post an ad there it also appears on the search engines. It really is free and quality advertising.

Social Media Sites

Popular social media sites include Facebook, Twitter, and LinkedIn. Once you set up an account with them under your business page, alert all your friends to follow your business and promotions. This may take a while to build adequate traffic to your site, but often you have to beg your friends and colleagues to support you this one time, or sometimes you might have to offer them a little incentive, like a gift certificate to their favorite coffee shop, restaurant, or bookstore.

Once your friends become responsive, ask them to send a message out to all of their friends. Include a coupon for discounts for anything on your website, including service. However, keep the amount conservative to increments of $5, $15, and $25 per responses who fill out the email contact form on your website.

Blogging

The idea behind blogging is that it allows you the opportunity to comment on issues of other bloggers while leading them to your website for more information, whether it relates to your products or your expertise.

Some of the most E-commerce blogs include:

- www.GetElastic.com
- www.GrooveCommerce.com
- www.BlueAcorn.com
- www.Retail-Ecommerce.com
- www.JohnChow.com
- www.PracticalEcommerce.com

Popular Informational Websites

There are several well-known sites that allow information article postings, such as ehow.com and wikipedia.com. These sites are quite helpful in getting your expertise recognized and trusted. The more you write and expose your business, the more people will look for your website to learn more about you and what you have to offer. I would caution you, however, to write only about topics related to your business, expertise, or experience.

Register with video sites that allow free postings and marketing. This is great because you can record yourself or testimonials about your product. Another thing to consider is finding videos that receive over a million views, and sending a message to the producer to negotiate a deal to have him put a link of your website at the bottom of the video. Trust me; it will drive insane traffic to your website. YouTube, for example, is the most popular site to post advertising videos for your business. Simply open an account and upload your videos to share your business ideas.

Advertising Techniques

No matter what kind of company you own, visibility is crucial. The easier it is for people to find your website, the more visitors you will be able to convert to clients. You must constantly create and manage an advertising campaign to attract web site traffic. Let's look at several elements that will work together to get the word out about your company:

1) **Forums and Groups:** Joining forums, Masterminds, or other groups that are related to your business is a fantastic avenue for building a customer data base. And you can find these groups for just about any topic imaginable.

2) **Word-of-Mouth.** Recommendations from satisfied friends, family or trusted web sites will generate more traffic for your business than you ever thought possible. Happy customers will continue to be the best advertisements for your business, and guess what; *it won't cost you a dime!*

3) **Keywords:** Keywords are words or short phrases associated with your business that people are most likely to use when they're looking for a company like yours. Ex. Carpet Cleaning...carpets, carpet cleaning, cleaning of carpets.

4) **Ezines and Newsletters:** An Ezine is basically a newsletter to keep potential customers reminded of your company's existence, but it is one of the most inexpensive, yet powerful forms of internet advertising

5) **Links:** Here are the three most popular forms of links:
   A) Inbound - A link leading to your site from another site that is not listed on yours
   B) Outbound - An external link from your site to another site that does not list yours on its pages
   C) Reciprocal - These links are round-robin pairs, and generally are posted when two web site owners agree to exchange links.

   But be careful - Posting unrelated links may smudge your professional image. Visitors may view your site as a dumping ground for links, and will be less likely to trust your legitimate content.

6) **Search Engine Submissions:** No matter how well your site is optimized, if search engines don't know your site exists, they will generally have a hard time finding it. There are several free web services that offer simultaneous submissions to multiple search engines. The more search engines your site is listed on, the more visitors you will receive.

7) **PPC (Pay-Per-Click) Campaigns.** Getting your web site to show up on the first page of results in a major search engine like Google, Yahoo or MSN can be a difficult and time-consuming process. Pay-per-click campaigns are one of the least expensive and most effective forms of internet advertising available. If you have ever used Google's search engine (and chances are if you use the

internet, you have), you may have noticed the links listed in a column along the right-hand side of the page. These links are the result of pay-per-click advertising campaigns.

8) **Autoresponders:** An autoresponder is an e-mail based program that does exactly what its name suggests: sends out an automatic response when an e-mail is received.

Chapter 11

Building Multiple Streams of Income

This section contains income opportunities that are turn-key in nature. Caution: The reason people fail in their attempts to start online businesses or home-based businesses is they don't expect to pay any more than the entrance fee in order to generate their desired income. The thing you have to understand about a Web-based business is that, just like any business, it takes time, money, and marketing/advertising efforts to generate revenue.

If you're not willing to pay at least $75–$150 per month to market your business, than please stop right here, because it takes money to make money. Don't look any further into starting a business because you will only set yourself up for failure. Otherwise, if you are willing to budget accordingly, then keep reading because you are in for a treat. I've compiled the most recent, hot money-making opportunities for online and home based businesses that will help you set up multiple streams of income.

I introduce to you the Red Hot Affiliate Programs—with an average payout of $25 to $200 per sale/referral. These involve a combination of free and low-cost sign-up.

To access the full list, please go to www.bizopps.mcbov.info. But for now, here is a short list of what is offered:

1. *Become an Affiliate*
   Learn what it means to become an affiliate and sell other peoples' products or information. The lists of products an affiliate can sell are endless. The best place to start is by visiting the website of the company and products of interest and click on their affiliate link. Another way to become an affiliate is by going to web portals (commission Junction or Click bank) listing affiliate opportunities for several companies at a time. This is

the most recommended way to get started to allow you to test your market. Go to **www.mcbov.info** for more info.

2. *Start your own craft business online*
   Learn what it takes to start your own craft business, whether you are skilled or not. If you are a natural when it comes to creating desirable crafts, then you are only steps away from turning it into a profitable business. The best way to start is by publishing pictures of your art work, open an ebay or craigslist account, and post your work and price and see if you get any responses or interested parties. Once you have finished testing your market, create a website to showcase your work. Another way to make money from craft, especially for those who have no experience, is to work with companies who hire work-from-home workers and train them how to make high demand crafts. This method not only allows you to start generating income, it will provide you with the skills necessary to start your own craft business down the line, while charging whatever amount you see fit. Go to **www.mcbov.info** for more info.

3. *Start a passive income Business as an Investor*
   Learn what it takes to earn passive income as an investor in tax lien certificates. Some investors are earning as high as a 24% interest on their money, so why not you, too? In a nutshell, the way this works is that every year or every other year the counties post in the papers properties that are delinquent in property tax payments for the year, including back taxes. A live auction is usually held at the county's administration location, and the property taxes are assigned to the lowest bidder on the interest earning potential. Go to *www.mcbov.info* for more info.

4. *Vending Machine Business*

Learn what you need to know to get started right away in the Vending Machine Business. For additional details, go to **mcbov.info** and look under Business Development Specialties.

www.myvendingsecret.com

5. *Start a Mail Order Business*

   Learn how to start your own mail order business selling how-to information and books. The best method of advertising for this type of business is by direct mailings and newspaper classified ads. This is a great business idea for those who are skilled writers with a heart for research and improvements. Go to **www.mcbov.info** for more info.

6. *Storage Auctions*

   This opportunity is all about generating income through storage auctions. When someone doesn't pay their rental fee, the owners of the storage facility cut off the lock and auction off all the items inside to the public.

   With my book Storage Auction Secrets, you're going to learn the inside techniques to getting items for the best price - and then you can resell them off-line or online for a massive profit!

   To learn more, go to **www.bizopps.mcbov.info.**

7. *Online Insurance Company*

   This is one of the best income opportunities right now, and I strongly recommend looking into it. See for yourself why this is the opportunity of a lifetime, and you can start your own online agency for less than $1,000, providing health, auto, life, and several other avenues of insurance right from the comfort of your home!

   www.bizopps.mcbov.info.

8. *Website Software*
   There's a whole world of possibilities in the software world for making money. For example, you can create them and provide them as products to other online businesses, or you can buy a bundle for your business and generate more money through the benefits. Find out more at **www.bizopps.mcbov.info.**

These are just a handful of different ideas for your next venture. If you would like more information on these, product reviews are available at **www.mcbov.info**.

The more streams of income you build for yourself, the more secure your future.

Chapter 12

Look Into The Crystal Ball

You have your vision for your company, or maybe you've already started it. So what happens in the next 6 months, 3 years, or 5 years? Where do you see your company going? Are you in it just for the short haul, make $100,000 and then move on? Do you want to just carve out a niche for yourself in the cupcake business, or do you want to be the number one global provider of cupcakes? Whatever your goals are for your company, you need to construct a solid plan to not only reach them, but to guide your business down the path of success.

Signed, sealed and delivered

You've probably never thought about this before but you need to have a "contract" when you are working with your personal and business goals. You can't just think about them and say you are going to accomplish them, because unfortunately you will forget them. So start by thinking about where you want to be in 5 years. Write your goal(s) down, and then work back to today. Having an "official" document will not only serve as a road map when you find that you are lost, but it is one fierce motivator.

Two good formats for you to use are contracts and proposals:

A. **Contract:** A very simple 1 or 2 page contract that states your business goals and intentions can be enough to start. Begin with the time commitment (part time, full time) that you plan to invest. Next, visualize what you eventually want your company to be, and the steps that you need to get there. Finally, sign and date your contract, and ask a family member or friend to sign as a witness. Have that person be an "accountability buddy" and check in with you from time to time to make sure that you are keeping on track.

B. **Proposal:** A proposal is more complicated than a contract, but if you take the time to write a great business proposal it will be well worth it for the detailed plan of action you end up with. Most business proposals document just about every piece of information important to your business, and can be several dozen pages long. A standard business proposal will include the following:

- *Business Description*: This is where you describe the industry and what your company's purpose is: products, sales, information or service.
- *Location*: Describe where and how your business is located (home office or storefront). Write down at least 5 benefits and downsides of operating your business from your location.
- *Management*: The management section features the resources, knowledge and experience that you (or you and your partner) bring to the company.
- *Personnel*: How many people will you need to hire? What will their duties be? Will they work part-time or full-time? Will they be hired on or sub-contractors?
- *Market*: Identify what part of the consumer population will be interested in your product or service.
- *Competition*: Research what other companies in your industry are doing, and note their strengths and weaknesses so that you can avoid making the same mistakes.
- *Financial data*: Calculate your income projection for the next few years. This will help to determine the best areas to concentrate your funds on.

- *Statement of Purpose*: This is a brief summary of your business goals that will serve as the framework for your document.
- *Business goals*: Expand on the points you mentioned in the Statement of Purpose. List everything you want to accomplish with your company.
- *Summary*: The summary ties everything together, and is a confirmation of your intentions.

Once you have everything written down, go back and make any changes that you need to. Once you are satisfied with the results, make a notation on your calendar for your first goal. On that day, take out your contract and proposal and make sure that you have accomplished what you set out to do, and cross it off your list. Move on to your next goal and give yourself a pat on the back.

"The secret of business is to know something that nobody else knows."

~Aristotle Onassis~

Chapter 13

Mindset Of An Entrepreneur

An entrepreneur is a person who assumes business responsibility and the risks that comes along with it. As an entrepreneur, one expects to make profits, whether big or small, depending on the business he or she is involved in. Generally speaking, the entrepreneur decides which product or service to offer, obtains the needed facilities, hires the required labor force, acquires production materials, and provides for the capital.

There is no assurance that any business will become a success. However, if the business proves to be a success, the entrepreneur will reap all the benefits and rewards in terms of the profits. In case of a loss, the entrepreneur will also be the one to suffer.

Only an experienced and knowledgeable individual will dare to become an entrepreneur.

Entrepreneurs are simply business people. Some people may think that it's really easy to become an entrepreneur, but they are very wrong. You see, there's more to just being called an entrepreneur. In fact, many studies are conducted by some experts to uncover the traits possessed by successful entrepreneurs.

What makes a successful entrepreneur? There are many factors that help in making an entrepreneur, like qualities, education, skills, and many others. There is, however, one thing that you shouldn't disregard if you want to become a victorious entrepreneur; mindset plays a very important role in the success of businesspeople.

Without mindset, you will definitely find it hard to succeed in whatever business endeavor you take on. To be one of the successful entrepreneurs, you must have the qualities needed to become one. You must know how to organize.

Entrepreneurs are often identified with how they look and think about things. According to many experts who studied various entrepreneurs, if you can think like an entrepreneur you have a high chance of succeeding in any form of business.

Successful entrepreneurs are positive thinkers. They always think that they can do everything. Confidence is one trait that you need to become an entrepreneur. You must have this trait as early as possible but don't worry if you're not that confident yet because you can still develop that just in time before you get involved in any business.

You must also be able to set your vision straight and look at certain situations differently. For ordinary individuals, problems are considered obstacles, but for many entrepreneurs, these are challenges. Aside from being a positive thinker, you must have a strong belief in your objectives. If you're confident enough, you can think straight at all times and you can set achievable objectives.

The business process is full of risks, and if you don't have the qualities of an entrepreneur, you will easily give in to such problems and obstacles. Being a risk taker is a very good trait of an entrepreneur. They are not afraid to be outside the so-called "safety zone." To succeed in any business undertaking, one must not be afraid of these risks.

However, you don't take risks blindly; you must be able to calculate them. By properly calculating the risks, you can determine if the risks are worth taking or not. If you think that by taking the risk you will gain more for the business, don't be afraid to accept it. If you don't put one foot forward, your business will not go anywhere.

Everything does not end in thinking alone. If you simply think and think, you will not achieve anything. But if you think and act, you will certainly reach the peak of success. Action is truly needed to put all your thoughts to action. You must be able to come up with well-intentioned objectives and your actions should be focused.

Now you know that the mindset of the individual is very important in order to become one of the successful entrepreneurs. If you think that you don't possess the proper mindset, you must learn to develop it as soon as possible, especially if you want to handle a business in the future.

By exerting some effort to develop your mindset, you can succeed. Being an entrepreneur is not that hard, especially if you possess the right qualities, skills, and most importantly – the proper mindset.

Characteristics of an Effective Entrepreneur

Before a doctor diagnoses a specific disease, his patient must undergo a series of laboratory exams and assessments. He has to know the history of his patient and how lifestyle affected his present health problem. As results come in, that would be an indication of the time when a physician gives specific drugs and therapies for maintenance. This will eventually contribute to the level of optimum health for that individual. If all else fails, the process will be repeated again.

Similar to what the abovementioned situation has stated, an entrepreneur's responsibility would be pretty much the same. It's just that he should see his customers as his patients and what they must have to survive a present predicament or a need. He must follow certain steps before doing anything irrational that could contribute to the downfall of his business. He should have certain instinctive characteristics in his personality because if he lacks any one of these, he's probably doomed to fail.

Entrepreneurship is collectively defined as exhibiting one's vision, taking action, and pursuing that vision as a goal to be achieved in life as service to reality. In the "quick and dirty" definition, it's getting your butt out of that couch and doing something rather than fulfilling your life's destiny of being a couch potato. Stated below are some of the distinct attitudes an entrepreneur should positively have:

- **Optimism:** Foreseeing things in a positive way, notwithstanding any circumstances that may hinder progress. The assertiveness of an individual depends on his knowledge of how to handle a difficult situation
- **Creativity:** Thinking outside the box. Expanding one's mind of what is beyond the ordinary through fine research and collection of data.
- **Stability:** Physical, mental, social or emotional, a leader must possess a stable life, which means he can handle tough situations during tough times.
- **Charisma:** Intelligence of communicating with different walks of life. Who says a charming man is less than an intelligent one? A good entrepreneur must have the certain magic glistening in his eyes, and can convey enchanting words to get hold of that convincing power no one dare resist.
- **Risk-taker:** As someone beginning his own dream, he should be stern and must have the guts to take the big leap of plunging into his own doom or success. He should not be afraid of taking chances when opportunity strikes.
- **Energetic:** Willing to do whatever it takes to reach the finish line. His drive for being an entrepreneur must always be at its highest level. His enthusiasm must exist for the next best thing to come along.

- **Time bound**: Like a written report in a newspaper, an entrepreneur must be on the top of every innovation. By looking at our past, we can predict our future.

Small businesses, in time, would turn out big if the scope of management exceeds what is expected. So it is necessary for a beginner to be positive about his endeavors. He must be very observant of what his environment lacks and needs. He should have sturdy shoulders to put on extra weight of carrying a responsibility that could change his or her life.

One's greatest failure is sticking with the mentality of being conventional. This would be one of an entrepreneur's greatest downfalls. Think Big. Act Big. Make your business dreams come true.

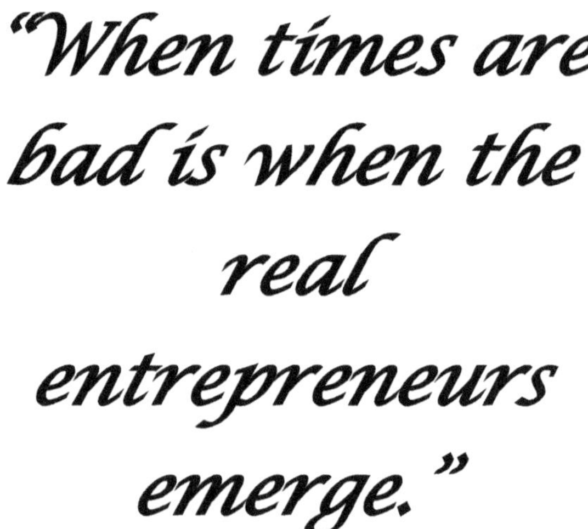
"When times are bad is when the real entrepreneurs emerge."
~Robert Kiyosaki~

Frequently Asked Questions

Let's dive right into some of the most common and significant questions you may have as you contemplate launching a new business:

Where will I get the money?

The start-up fund is a common concern when starting a business. However, the thing you need to understand about success is that the first step is to know what you want, believe that you can achieve it, and be ready to receive it.

Once you are confident, the next step is to meditate on the idea with a clear mind until you receive a clear plan. Practice visualizing what you want, write it down to remind yourself of what you want, and share it with others.

Join a group or club of like-minded people, and when your heart is ready, you will be amazed at how things fall into place. The money will come once you have a clear idea of what you've envisioned, you have it written on paper (in the form of a business plan or strategic plan), you've done your research, and your ideas make good business sense.

Typical funding sources are bank loans, network connections, angel loans, grants, family members, franchise loans, affiliate sales, or donations.

What if I don't know much about business—how do I get started?

In the beginning, I had no clue what running a business involved, especially how to market it. My first experience occurred in high school when I worked as a retail sales associate. I was not only expected to sell clothing, but also to offer the store credit cards. These were believed to increase sales, based on the notion that people tend to spend more with a store credit card than with cash or a major credit card. By signing up at least twenty-five customers per month, I became one of the top sales associates. I worked there for almost four years, and then I left that job to sell makeup for one of the most recognized independent contractor companies. The company had different methods for selling its products, such as door to door, passing out samples to friends and family, and purchasing the products for ourselves on a monthly basis. After one year, I left the makeup company to join a well-known network marketing company that incorporated all the previous products that I had sold before including clothing, makeup, shoes, home products, and nutritional products.

Unfortunately, by the end of my experiment, I was still clueless. It was not until I started reading business books at my local bookstores that I truly began to understand the ins and outs of running a business profitably. I learned even more after going to graduate school to earn my MBA. The most valuable lesson I learned from the MBA program involved managerial economics.

How do I know I will make it?

A pertinent question often raised by experts is why many businesses fail in the first five years. Starting a business is not for everyone. It takes a risk taker who is willing to do whatever it takes to make things work. Business has its rewards when done right. The lifeblood of business success includes accurate budgeting, forecasting, marketing, advertising, and managing people and resources.

One thing I recommend is to have more than one partner who can fill in your weaknesses. Whether it's in finance, marketing, project management, or legal, as an entrepreneur, it's very beneficial to stay plugged in with local business clubs, to attend seminars, and to read books relating to business, success, and new innovations.

What do I need to consider when starting a business from scratch?

After reading this book you should have a better understanding of determining the start-up costs, potential earnings, typical fees, advertising methods and costs, your qualifications, equipment needed, home-based business potential, staff required, how to account for your weaknesses, how to account for hidden cost, down sides versus up sides, and the fundamental basis for your business idea.

For more help, go to the form on my website at **www.member.mcbov.info** and login to receive access to my "Business Database" spreadsheets, calculate potential start-up expenses, and input your future business performance projections.

"Everyone has an invisible sign hanging from their neck saying, 'Make me feel important.' Never forget this message when working with people."

~Mary Kay Ash~

Helpful Hints

Helpful Hints

HELPFUL HINT #1: Determine your motivations for running a company right from the start: "I want to be here for my family," or "I'm sick of dazzling clients left and right just to make my boss look good," or "If gas prices rise one more time, I'll have to start riding a bike to work." Then commemorate those motivations in physical form: make a poster, use the marquee setting on your computer's screensaver, or write it with a marker on a coffee mug. Keep your driving force on display at your home office desk and glance at it every once in a while—like after you've just argued with a client over why he should pay the invoice you sent him thirty days ago, or while you're up at two in the morning trying to put the finishing touches on a proposal. It will remind you why you're doing this, and what your rewards are.

HELPFUL HINT #2: Set a schedule for yourself and stick to it. Because you are working for yourself, you have the ability to create a flexible schedule that fits around the rest of your life. Perhaps you are able to devote the hours of 9 to 5 for work. Or, if you're following a model in order to spend time with your family, you may choose to work while the kids are at school, and then put in a few more hours at the end of the day, after they've gone to bed. You can give yourself weekends off, or schedule additional hours on the weekends in order to have more free time during the week. Whatever schedule you set for yourself, the only important thing is to make sure you follow it as strictly as possible so you're not scrambling to get things done.

HELPFUL HINT #3: If you're able, have two separate computers: one for work, and one for leisure. One of the most difficult challenges in running a company is setting boundaries between work and personal time; more often than not, beginners blend everything together and end up feeling like every waking moment is spent working. Having separate computers helps you distinguish work from leisure in your mind, and allows you to maintain your professional side while still finding time to unwind. Do not install instant messenger programs, chat room applets or computer games on your workstation computer; save those for private time.

HELPFUL HINT #4: Are you hopeless at writing? Do your designs resemble disaster scenes? If you feel you cannot create professional-looking web pages and clear, effective web copy, don't be afraid to hire a freelancer to do it for you. Writing and graphic design are the two largest industries that use freelancers, and there are hundreds of thousands of people who make a living through contracted writing and design services. Your company is worth the one-time cost of hiring a freelancer to do the job right the first time.

HELPFUL HINT #5: It's great to be able to store practically your entire business on one electronic device. The one problem you might encounter is this: *Your entire business is stored on one electronic device.* If your computer crashes or breaks, you could be out of business for weeks while you get a new system and try to recover your files. Therefore, it is **imperative** that you back up your system regularly, and store the backup files in some place other than your home office. The best idea is to keep them at a location other than your home, such as the home of a relative or friend. That way you're covered in case of loss, and you'll be able to reopen your business as fast as possible.

About the Author

About The Author

Born in Port au Prince, Haiti, Michele Beauvoir came to the United States at the age of eleven. Living in Evanston, Illinois, she quickly learned English, and in high school she took a job at Sears as a sales associate in the clothing department, where she learned how to communicate effectively and influence buyers' decisions. After high school, she attended Oakton Community College and earned her associate degree. She worked for Avon, Mary Kay, and Amway until she took a two-month trip to Gonaïve, Haiti as a public relations intern. While in Haiti, she began to write out a strategic plan for building an enterprise, and upon her return she started a housekeeping business.

In 2006 Michele went back to school to earn her bachelor's degree in biomed at National University of Health Sciences, and then to Rockford College in Rockford, Illinois, where she earned her MBA.

McBov REI, which Michele founded in 2008, started as a real estate investment company in the area of property auctions. The company became registered in 2009 and expanded services online in the area of real estate investment and entrepreneurial coaching. Today, McBov REI has expanded to include business start-up development and marketing services. Michele is the founder of Home Based Business LLC. Other successful businesses founded by Michele include McBov's Affordable

Contractors LLC for home and office cleaning, handyman, and repair services, as well as ghostwriting services, web designing, and copywriting.

Michele provides valuable information to stimulate entrepreneurial creativity in business start-ups and investment opportunities. For Support and Consulting Help call (888) 948-3247 or visit the main website or blog at **www.mcbov.info.**

Send all inquiries to
McBOV REI, Inc
PO Box 582
Belvidere, IL 61008

"Success is liking yourself, liking what you do, and liking how you do it."

~Maya Angelou~

www.ingramcontent.com/pod-product-compliance
Lightning Source LLC
Chambersburg PA
CBHW051325170526
45166CB00002B/686

9781492878469